T0194711

Zola Discovers South Africa's

TEEN YEARS

by Alexandria Pereira

AuthorHouse™
1663 Liberty Drive
Bloomington, IN 47403
www.authorhouse.com
Phone: 833-262-8899

Because of the dynamic nature of the Internet, any web addresses or links contained in this book may have changed since publication and may no longer be valid. The views expressed in this work are solely those of the author and do not necessarily reflect the views of the publisher, and the publisher hereby disclaims any responsibility for them.

This book is printed on acid-free paper.

ISBN: 978-1-6655-6554-7 (sc)
ISBN: 978-1-6655-6553-0 (hc)
ISBN: 978-1-6655-6552-3 (e)

Library of Congress Control Number: 2022913212

Print information available on the last page.

Published by AuthorHouse 08/15/2022

authorHOUSE®

Zola Discovers South Africa's

by Alexandria Pereira

AuthorHouse™
1663 Liberty Drive
Bloomington, IN 47403
www.authorhouse.com
Phone: 833-262-8899

Because of the dynamic nature of the Internet, any web addresses or links contained in this book may have changed since publication and may no longer be valid. The views expressed in this work are solely those of the author and do not necessarily reflect the views of the publisher, and the publisher hereby disclaims any responsibility for them.

This book is printed on acid-free paper.

ISBN: 978-1-6655-6554-7 (sc)
ISBN: 978-1-6655-6553-0 (hc)
ISBN: 978-1-6655-6552-3 (e)

Library of Congress Control Number: 2022913212

Print information available on the last page.

Published by AuthorHouse 08/15/2022

authorHOUSE®

The Mystery of History Series

South Africa

Book 3 of 4

Dedication

To my grandma, whose life work was dedicated
to children and their pursuit of knowledge.

"Grandma, what are you cooking?" asked Zola.

"I am making Malay Curry for dinner tonight," replied Grandma.

"Hum! Could we learn more about our South African history today?" asked Zola.

"Yes, Zola. I thought you might want to learn more, so I brought out my South African history book for us to look at," said Grandma.

"Oh Cool! Thanks, Grandma!" said Zola.

"People called San, Khoekhoe, and Bantu lived in South Africa for many thousands of years. They hunted, gathered, and farmed for their food, and raised their children. South Africa grew and grew.

Then about 600 years ago, people from the continent of Europe started coming to South Africa. First came sailors from the country of Portugal, but they did not stay.

"Then came sailors from the country of the Netherlands. We call them the Dutch. They landed their big ships at the Cape of Good Hope on their way to the continent of Asia to trade. Some of the Dutch sailors decided to stay in South Africa and built small houses, in small groups called colonies.

"A big company called the Dutch East India Trading Company started to trade with South Africa. Their big ships brought things like cotton and copper to trade for gold and ivory.

"Later, more people, called Afrikaners, came from countries like Germany and France. Many became farmers, called 'Boers'. Boer means farmer in the Dutch language. The Boers built farms that grew and grew and took up a lot of land - land that was already being used by the San and Khoekhoe people to hunt and gather. They did not want to give the land to the farmers. This created conflicts and arguments between people.

"Then came people from the country of the United Kingdom, called the British.

The British people built more colonies, on San and Khoekhoe land, but they only wanted British, Boer, and Afrikaner people to live in them.

The Boers needed help from the San and Khoekhoe people to build and work on their growing farms. This created even more conflicts and arguments between people, even though the people worked hard and the farms grew and grew.

"Over time the British and Boers continued to have a hard time working together. They could not agree on a government or rules that worked for them both. So about 200 years ago, a lot of Boer families packed up all the things in their house and moved east, away from the colonies. It was called the Great Trek. By working together to solve problems, the Boers made a new life for themselves away from the British.

"When diamonds and gold were discovered, inside the Vredefort crater, created when a meteorite hit earth before people or animals lived, South Africa changed again.

"Mines and factories were built, to find those diamonds and gold, to make more things to trade. People from the countries of Angola and Ghana came to South Africa to do this work.

Money earned from trading diamonds, gold, and coal, paid to build roads, railroads, and big cities. People from the country of India came to South Africa to build those things.

These people were not paid or treated well, but all these people who mined, and built factories, roads, and big cities helped South Africa grow," said Grandma.

"But Grandma, what happened to the San people?" asked Zola.

"The San people continued to walk north over many hundreds of years until they found a place that was difficult for others to get to. This place is called the Kalahari Desert. There they built their small mud and grass huts, raised their animals, and hunted and gathered for their food. The San people felt safe there, and by working together, they continued to live just as they have for many thousands of years.

"Ever since the Dutch sailors first landed in South Africa, the governments and rules of South Africa have been changing. First the Dutch made the government and rules, then the British, then the Dutch again, and then the British again.

When the British finally let the people of South Africa make their own government, the government, and the rules they made, did not keep the people safe or help the people work together.

"For forty years, people fought each other over how the government and rules were made. Many people worked hard trying to change the government so it would make rules that would help people work together to solve problems. Two men named Nelson Mandela and Desmond Tutu worked hard trying to make this change. The government was mean to them and tried to stop them. But they never gave up.

Mr. Mandela and Mr. Tutu each asked for help from people in other countries. The people in those countries told the government of South Africa it had to change its rules so that all its people could be safe and work together. If it did not, those countries would not be friends with the government of South Africa.

"About thirty years later, the South African government finally listened and allowed most of the people to help make the government and its rules. A new leader, F.W. de Klerk, helped make rules that were good for all the people of South Africa. Mr. Mandela, Mr. Tutu, and Mr. de Klerk helped the government and people of South Africa work together to solve problems. Then the people of South Africa could learn new things, have new ideas, and grow," said Grandma.

"Wow, Grandma! For a long time, it was hard for people to get along. Our ancestors worked hard to work together, solved conflicts, formed a government, and made rules so everyone could grow. I thank my ancestors for working hard so that I can be here today learning about our South African history," said Zola.

"We will finish the story of our South African history tomorrow. It's time for dinner now. Can you help me set the table please?" asked Grandma.

"Sure, and thank you, Grandma," said Zola.

"You are welcome," said Grandma.

Educational Support Activities for Adults to Engage with Children

Basic Human Needs
We need food to grow.
We need clothing to keep us warm.
We need shelter to keep us safe and dry.
We need to socialize to work together.
We need to solve problems so we can invent and be creative.

Practical Life and Sensorial Foundation
Plant a seed. Go on a berry hunt. Why do these things?

History
Use a timeline to show and ask what happened: past, present, and future.

Science
Build a model of a mud and grass hut.
Paint rocks using crushed charcoal and natural pigments, like berries; use twigs for brushes.

Geography and Map Work
Find the Continent of Africa on a map. Find South Africa on the African Continent.
Trace South Africa and draw significant landforms, mountains, rivers, plateaus, beaches, etc. Draws lines of migration into South Africa.

Language
Make up a new language using signs or clicks. What are you saying?

Earth Science
How do we learn about the solar system from meteorites that land on earth?

South African Timeline for Adult Reference

3 million BC	The first human ancestors, the *Australopithecus afarensis*, appear in the Cradle of Humankind, situated in today's South Africa.
300,000 BC - 300 AD	First *Homo sapiens* inhabited parts of South Africa.
1488 AD	Portuguese explorer Bartolomeu Dias sails around the southern tip of Africa, the Cape of Good Hope, and Khoekhoe establish trade with Europeans.
1497	Vasco da Gama arrives at the Cape of Good Hope on his way to India.
1500's	Portuguese ships land at Table Bay. The Bantu farmers and herdsmen establish trade with the Europeans.
1652	The Dutch East India Company establishes the Dutch Cape Colony.
1663	More European sailors establish a settlement at Saldanha Bay.
1795	The British take control of Cape Colony.
1802	The Dutch regain control of Cape Colony.
1806	The British regain control of Cape Colony.
1814	The Dutch formally give the Cape to Britain.
1833	The Great Trek begins, as 6,000 Dutch settlers, called Boers, migrated eastward from the Cape Colony.
1867	Diamonds are discovered in the Orange Free State at Kimberley.
1885	The Cape-to-Kimberley railroad was completed.
1886	Gold is discovered and the Witwatersrand Gold Rush starts.
1893 - 1914	Mahatma Gandhi started his nonviolent, noncompliance methods helping India's working in the Transvaal protest against the government's Pass Laws, Black Act.

1934	The Status of the Union Act declares South Africa's independence from the United Kingdom.
1948	Apartheid begins in South Africa.
1961	The Republic of South Africa is established, quitting the British Commonwealth.
1961	UN General Assembly refuses to recognize South Africa.
1962	UN General Assembly calls for sanctions against South Africa. Nelson Mandela announces a campaign of sabotage against government buildings.
1967	World's first heart transplant operation was conducted by South African surgeon Dr. Barnard.
1984	Desmond Tutu wins Nobel Peace Prize.
1989	Work begins to end apartheid. People of all races vote in parliamentary elections.
1990	Nelson Mandela is released from prison.
1992	Most European sanctions lifted. UN General Assembly ends certain restrictions.
1993	Most UN sanctions lifted. Constitution of the Republic of South Africa ratified.
1994	Apartheid is fully repealed. First democratic national election held. Nelson Mandela was elected president.
2015	South African government makes rules in an attempt to give farmland back to black farmers.
2019	Women were appointed to half the government's cabinet posts in South Africa.

Printed in the United States
by Baker & Taylor Publisher Services